the Judgement:
Awakened by Thunder into triumph!
Awakened by Thunder: terror, then laughter!
Terror for a thousand li! The wise man
does not release the sacred spoon
or mishandle the chalice of life.

the Image:
Thunder twice! Awakened by terror: thus
with hopeful dread, the wise man
orders his outer life according to truth,
and examines his immortal soul.

—The Book of Changes

For while the Plough tips round the Pole
The trained mind outs the upright soul

As Jesus said the trained mind might
Being wiser than the sons of light

But trained men's minds are spread so thin
They let all sorts of darkness in

Whatever light man finds they doubt it
They love not light, but talk about it

—John Masefield

for Reginald Leon Blount
whose life is a *Book of Changes*

Now a Major Motion Picture
by Joshua Alan Sturgill

Catalog Number 016
ISBN: 979-8-9863904-2-0

Publisher's Cataloging-in-Publication data

Names: Sturgill, Joshua Alan, author.
Title: Now a major motion picture : poetry in dialogue with the Book of Changes / by Joshua Alan Sturgill.
Description: Cochiti Lake, NM: Darkly Bright Press, 2023
Identifiers: ISBN: 979-8-9863904-2-0
Subjects: LCSH Poetry, American. | American poetry--21st century. | Yi jing--Poetry. | BISAC POETRY / American / General | POETRY / Subjects & Themes / Animals & Nature | POETRY / Subjects and Themes / Inspirational & Religious
Classification: LCC PS3569.T87 N69 2023 | DDC 811.6--dc23

darkly bright
press & design

www.darklybrightpress.com

Now A Major Motion Picture

Poetry in dialogue with the *Book of Changes*

NOW
A MAJOR
MOTION PICTURE

Poetry in dialogue with the Book of Changes

Joshua Alan Sturgill

Darkly Bright Press

1   PULSE

the Heart
& the Moon speak
with one voice

in language
of pulses & tides
they say

      inward
is upward. Inward
is Upward

Perhaps a spectrographic sequencing
to calculate nutrition in her skin
or firm genetic evidence will yield
a clearer picture of the subject's fate.

The convolutions of her brain [as here
in figure 36] are clearly seen
beneath a flaxen knot of hair, locks curled
and reddened by the acids of the bog.

The cloth [in figure 37] tied
across her eyes to blind her, closely spun
from strands of wool, had been a scarf or some
adornment worn to indicate her age

—we might note this extraordinary use
for such an ordinary thing. Thus bound
and blinded, naked, weighted by a rock,
the subject is preserved beneath the peat

for eighteen hundred years. Though scientists
and specialists construct scenarios
in explanation of her death, a wealth
of questions still remain which can't be solved.

See how [in figure 38] the face
bears an expression patient and resigned.
And while her other bones (though calcified)
retain their shape, we note

the dissolution of her ribs: enough
        to leave the heart exposed

Stars are scattered
shards of Adam's bones
in bright anticipation

burning. My eyes
touch them; I taste
twilight's cloud of salt;

rivers of memory
still flow from Eden
where I had no need

for memory. I ate
stillness at the Altar.
Who measures Adam's

lamentation? Night,
that vast reliquary
of lights observed & lines

suggested — cyphers
of a spacious language
we no longer speak

yet stand within

When I mastered the use of the yardstick,
I asked *how many gallons is the ocean?*

But when I graduated to the metric system
I found the sea is really liters. Look:

the stars! So much hydrogen burning.
And night? A trick of earth's rotation.

And planets, too. They look just like stars
except in photographs. Planets are stones

spinning, like earth. So there are many
"earths," statistically. To reach them

only takes a bit of time. Time is measured
by a year, and that makes distance easy:

simply add kilometers to years. Now,
with measures made of measures,

everything's in reach. Those other earths
are usable, no more or less than mine

I'll step now down among the meadowsweet
and rest its tannic resin on my tongue. Confuse
my thoughts with snowmelt streams, my fingers
for the smaller branches of the bramble oaks.

I'll step now down into the breath of sunlight,
tangled in the lupine and the larkspur sprays. I'll find
my eyes are reading mountain meadows, just as if
the grasses and the wildflowers were a score

of music. Drinking deeply, I'll discern the oldest texts
of native ways: ten thousand generations hunting deer
on paths the deer themselves have made. This hill,
a paragraph—each pebble is a word from volumes

stacked in shale cliffs—will tell how Heaven
lives beneath the Earth as well, supporting Earth
with burnished hands, face raised and radiant
with expectation. Earth's enlightenment is Heaven's

contemplation. When my eyes are full, I'll step now
blindly, down among the river stones. And while
I walk, I feel the laughing cold of ice released
—a myth my bare, brave feet will read to me

We argued in the kitchen. And by accident
you cut your hand, gesticulating with the knife
to punctuate some comment that you thought
would prove you right beyond all doubt

beyond all doubt you said, and when you
dropped the knife, I watched with some alarm
as points of fact (the ones you tried to hide
behind your argument) swelled out

swelled hugely from the wound like shining
insects. Darkly opalescent ants came filing
out across the countertop, antennae waving
anxiously ahead of them in search of dark

in search of shelter, scattering along
the mugs, the cutting board, the silverware
and hiding in your mother's antique plates.
I gaped and gasped, but you ignored them

you ignored or didn't see them, just kept
jabbing at the air with words, while I'm repulsed
but mesmerized by bobbing legs and swinging
mandibles. They look like all our arguments

our years of arguments about unnecessary things
(or sometimes necessary, too, but always competition,
always rushed). And now the ants are climbing
on your face—*but wait, I'm nearly finished*

nearly done, you say as I step back and mutely
point and stare. Your eyes (they're all that I
can see) seem fixed on arguing. *I'm right
again*, you say, *where are you going now?*

*You're leaving now? Just when you see
what I've been saying all along? Just when
the truth is clear to you?* But I can only
answer: yes, the truth. It's finally clear

You know
better than most
how bitter doctrine can be

as you finish
your breakfast ramen, the
Institutes or the

Manifesto open
on your dorm room floor.
You ingest

by imposed necessity
these packaged lists
of belief; yours

is an intellect tasked
with finding essentials
and cultivating a taste

for attack. A system
is all you need. It may
be dry, it may be

over-salted. *But that's
just how it is* you say.
No, it isn't

fresh from the
Garden. But it keeps
long past the war

When the cast-bronze Dancing
Shiva was explained to me, I wept

because I recognized You beneath
a new disguise. I saw the universe

tangled with your hair, your feet
still glistening with spikenard

and blood. All the burning arms
by which You love me, I keep closely

as the caverns and the gospels of
my heart. And I've learned now

why I'm blind. I looked too long
within Your Wheel. I thought I

could fool You into finding me. *I'll
be an echo in an empty room* I said,

to lure You in with curiosity. But
who was tricked? To whose delight?

The voice, the vacancy, the walls were
You—You there already, ever-moving,

motionless. I sprang. I bound. I'll soar.
I long for each unveiling. I am forever

wild with doubled-headed drums
and rhythmic fire, deaf to cries from

ignorance, dancing where the Ganges
and the Ganges of the Sky

behold their single Source.
You fashioned from Yourself

a whip of snakes; You overturned
the world; pigeons and cattle flew

out of everything, mad with fright,
released into their freedom

June is National Kidney Stone Awareness Month.
Our office has been putting in extra hours to make

this year's campaign the most successful yet! You'll
soon see billboards with the slogan *Know the Signs*

(which we chose over *Small Things Sometimes
Cause Big Problems*, due to length) captioning

the photograph of an elderly-yet-athletic man
whose face expresses intelligent concern.

We've planned a mass mailing to addresses
provided by healthcare professionals, a website

and a 1-800 hotline for symptom inquiries.
Awareness is the first step. Are you at risk

for urolithiasis? Do you *Know the Signs?*
When you call, our volunteer representatives

will be happy to tell you the signs in June. June
is National Kidney Stone Awareness Month

Some orient their lives by lines
on paper maps, and some by signs
they leave along the roads they walk.
And many think by precepts taught

in classrooms under artificial light.
But I am lost and late until the night
reveals the Stars. What better clock?
What better guide? A door unlocked,

a window wide upon the Real East
—horizon of an endless Feast!
The East of compass turning? No,
an ever-East where dawn is burning

always on the Planets and the Moon,
who blush, embarrassed, drunk at noon.
Through courtyards of chronology
they dance! In ballrooms of ontology

they sing with spiraled inspiration,
sounding silent invitations: *Come*
and dine with us! Drink from our cup!
They never cease to call: *Come in! Come up!*

But here below, most think of money spent,
distracted, anxious for the next event;
while others, wounded, seek relief.
They bless a moment free from grief.

> I'm bound by Earth as well. But I
> am like a lake that yet reflects the sky.

I navigate the labyrinth of geography
by reference to celestial cartography,
and even as my death completes my birth,
I take to heart the heavens' immortal mirth

Someone once told me
of a Taoist sage, a hermit, who

cast his divinations on bare earth
with three plum stones. How

did he mark them to distinguish
Yang sides from Yin? I wondered

with respectful curiosity. Though
I suspect such marks would prove
unnecessary. I've met other sages

in other lands; I knew them
by their ageless gaze. Intuition
intimate as touch, they could ask

How so? even from the silence
of a seed, and hear the answer
with half-closed eyes

I wondered, with respectful curiosity

When the Monsters migrate
grazing slow and heavy overhead
through forests of the Old Answers,
sap from wounded stems
spills down, spattering
the paint and plaster of our cities
with glints of the sky.

      And our children,
their attention revived by hoofbeats
of thunder, lift their ivory lattices,
eyes wide and limbs pale, and ask
Who makes the taste of rain?
What language does the Moon speak?
Where does skin for clothing come from,
and the bone for toys? But since

      we fear our children
might see monsters or find the Sun
in shining puddles, we read to them
from the dung-paper picture books
which contain The Ceremony of Drought.
We chant the litanies and hymns;
we tell the stories *Once upon a time*
there was a Noise and *It's from stones*
the leather and the paper grow.

      We show the children
how the mountains are dissected,
how rivers of ideas are set
in concrete courses. *Old Answers,*
weren't they lovely? we say, *but*
New Surmisings give us everything
we use. As we close the lattices
to make night again,

we sing our children
a Ceremonial Rhyme to help them fall
asleep:

Skies deceive us; light has lied.
Dust must daily be applied.
What are monsters?
What are moons?
Games for rainy afternoons.

Then, with handfuls of earth
we dull the sap that shimmers
on the horn tiles of our doorsteps, and
pray the monsters
soon depart

Janie, I miss you. I miss you so fiercely. Remember the Milky Way winding above us like some cosmic rainbow? So distant, you said, that the colors get lost in their flying from out there to Kansas, to where we were. Here we are still (well, at least in my memory) telling our dreams as we sit on the trampoline, stargazing, laughing, amazed at our honesty. Daydreams, you claimed, are the most honest part of us.

Janie, I miss you. I'm older, but I'm still the same soul you recognized—old souls are old friends, you quoted—and all that you told me, I haven't forgotten. With everything else, I remember distinctly: you told me

The Moon is a Woman

You said this with confidence, swore by the sky, and the gravelly caw of a raven and wind in the hackberry echoed *it's true*. You had five explanations, five proofs you'd discovered. The first was her *Mystery* (mystery's what we can always know more of). Then something of *Thought* (you said thought is a flame, and the nature of flame is to fly up to heaven). Then something of *Phases* and *Darknesses* (not every dark is the same, you insisted).

So: Mystery, Thought, Phases, Darknesses. What was the last? Some alchemical image—recalling a memory lost? Or persistence of Truth, though it tarnishes? Yes: the Moon's likeness to *Silver*—her vividness veiled, but never removed

mystery's what we can
always know more of

Imagine with me
I have invented a Tool, a means
to accomplish the perfect Art.

All things are its medium. It leaves
no pollution, no residue, no remainder,
because it remakes all things

into what they are: stars
into angels, water into blood, stones
interpret the sea. Mountains

are the letters of its alphabet.
While I work, time halts,
patient as the canvas

under the painter's brush. My Tool
binds all things together: all tree,
all portrait, every surface

a window.
            Then, imagine with me
I teach my children the secrets

of my Tool. We become a family
of craftsmen, the great artisans
of history. Yet we leave

no monuments, no lasting cities.
Our Art is strong enough
to be intangible. Tuned

to silence. Obvious, unobserved.
            Imagine the effect
of the Tool on the human soul.

From my children's children, verity
is respired like the blue haze
rising from a mountain lake

on a Summer dawn. Without
coercion, they come to us
to be named: insects

and galaxies, the whole Cosmos
aching to be dressed
in saffron and ermine and gold

You were sitting alone in your car, convenience
store sandwich half-finished in your hand, half-

watching the birds, when the Revelation reached you.
Before today, you'd always ignored their donut-crumb

economy carried out among the phantom shapes
of oil stains. Scavengers, you said. *Stop-N-Go*

vagabonds. You're an experienced traveler. You paused
for fuel and food per your routine when their urgent

modesty arrested you. Their unpretentious nests
above the mercury lights and in the crook of the *-N-*

revealed this old gas station suddenly as someone's
home. With peaceful instantaneity, you learn

one beggar may say to another when alms are scarce,
God give you what you need. And this means *may you*

not be one who suffers today. Amen is the reply,
comparing past losses, darkly noting the erratic paths

of passing cars. Your classroom is the quiet solitude
of your car; your teacher is a pigeon with a fishing

line tangled in her feathers, standing ungainly at the
Exit/Entrance, outside the curve defined by *To Remain*

Open During Business Hours. You watch her leap
through meteors of shoppers' legs; she risks, clasps

and rises in painfully disheveled dips of wings, bearing
in her beak a triumphant kernel of orange-powdered

popcorn, a bright but meager meal. The lesson is
simply: to observe how life survives on nothing

missed by hurried travelers, routinely fueling, talking,
spilling food. And looking at yourself, you see crumbs

from your sandwich fallen on your lap. But crumbs
are topaz and celandines. How did you not know?

There can't be beauty here you might have believed
before the Revelation came. Now afternoon speaks

to you in the advertising banners; colors leap out
of the broken sidewalk, music from a shrub

ensouled with sparrows. You open the door. *God
give you what you need* you say, and priest-like

lift your hands to brush a little of your bread
among the oil stains before you drive away

I stop digging

I stand in my grave
unfinished

now I am a tree, I said

I am made of hands

bury your feet
next to mine

drink from my grave

our heart shares
secret rivers. We

are a forest
unfinished

our heart shares secret rivers

I've decided eggs
are logically impossible.
Because birds are not only not round,
but soft and angular. Nearly the inverse

of eggs. Let go an egg, it moves
in a direction opposite that of a bird.
And this unnaturally perfect Form
emerges without precedent, contrary

to logical expectation. So I've decided
the making of eggs in the bodies of birds
is related to their (the birds') frequent
approaches to the Sun.

Hear me out on this, because
when science fails, myth
must kindly intervene.
What perfect circles are found in nature?

        1. The Sun
        2. The Moon
        3. The Iris and pupil of an eye
        4. Eggs

There may be round flowers and fruits,
but their roundness is malleable,
rarely flawless. Eggs are impractically
perfect, useless against this world

of vicissitude. We might define vicissitude:
        1. A hard surface
        2. Gravity
        3. Any combination of 1 & 2

So I suspect birds bring something
back from the Sun—something ethereal,
celestial.   Something necessarily resembling
orbits and epicycles. Hence, eggs.

Now, I've already considered (you may have
as well) that reptiles also bear eggs, so that
birds and lizards are somehow akin.
May I suggest this as another instance of

AS ABOVE, SO BELOW—that reptiles
borrowed the egg from birds,
who received it from the sky. But reptiles
don't know how to care for this gift.

They abandon their eggs—afraid
of what they've done—afraid, perhaps
because they've brought these
Symbols of the Sun
          unawares,
                    into the cold
of the dark places they prefer

[A SONNET FROM A DAMAGED MANUSCRIPT]

...who studies them with care   will soon observe
Her secret tongue   at once antique and new
Yet linked by strands   of focused thought, that serve
The stone is as the mountain   Silver-hued

where, hemorrhaged   by storms or deserts lined
Stirred   suddenly to life!   by rite, perform
companions of the Moon   the Moon-lit mind
           A movement of the outmost toward the Form

These mystic incantations, said aloud
or wordless mystery.   Together, take
a balance?   then, the pillar and the cloud
            Their fragile union, all to mend or break

Contained herein: a record of the Way
  which, once embraced   She never can decay

she never can decay

I onced lived in the open West
where there are valleys still
without artificial light, without
trains or highways, just lonely
gravel roads like pale ribbons
tangled in the mountains.

I remember driving home from work
one night, exhausted, with my mind
still caught on tasks unfinished,
when suddenly I saw the Sign
of an Apocalypse in the broad
dark sky above the mountains.

Moonless, cloudless, the stars
were thick enough to grey the heavens
one hue lighter than the graphite
of the trees, when, into the expanse,
a fantastic Orange flared up and out
of everything. Forest, sky, mountains

flamed and flickered, began to glow
like ghostly candles, like a dawn
at nearly midnight settling in waves
of incandescent glare. I stopped the car
because I feared I might be driving toward
a forest fire galloping down the mountains

and stepped out to better see the source
of all this eerie light. Every tree, stone,
flower and hillside ruddy and smoldering.
I looked up, spellbound, and, speeding
down from space, a meteor (almost,
I thought, a planet!) blazed
a fiery light on every mountain

—a meteor gargantuan, and breaking
into pieces as it fell. What takes a minute
to describe happened fast, as quickly
as the dark returned, leaving lightning
branded in my eyes. I waited
for a BOOM, for some explosion
or an earthquake in the mountains.

    But all was still. And slowly,
    nighttime noises dared to speak
    again: an owl, and the murmur
    of a little stream beside the road.

There are valleys still, where you
can see forewarnings in the sky, where
no one walks the roads for days,
where the End hasn't yet begun,
because Beginning still breathes there
and wonders are revealed there
among the watchful mountains

In my parallel life
I am a figure skater.
I propel
the craft of skating
beyond athletics

into a realm
of metaphysical art.
I make skating
a language;
I enrapture

my audience
with a performance
both explosive and
intimate, a shadow
spinning in a zoetrope:

see many-rayed Venus
rise, awake before dawn,
or is this
the mimicry
of a wild horse

flying up
from a dark ravine?
But then, by
spinning combined
with a rhythmic

arching of my arms,
the spectacle altogether
leaves representation
and bursts
into the complex

beauty
of an arabesque,
a gestured geometry,
an offering of names
to the Nameless.

My audience sees
only signals, only images
centrifugal and imprecise.
But within myself:
I contemplate

the flavor
of an overripe orange.
The sensuality of its oil
in its tight skin, biting
and pungent in

the cumbrous heat
of an August afternoon
          —a contrast
to the ice beneath me
nearly absolute

I delight to be deceived
by superficiality. I care only
for the taste and disregard
the meaning of my words.

I naively love *limpidity*
as much as *ambiguity*,
with no wish to distinguish

souvenir from *parasite*
ephemeral from *salience*
abundance from *effluvia.*

What does it matter what
they *mean*? So many sharp
and shining syllables!

Why can't I eat them all
—and interchangeably?
No one any more believes
oblivion is *hazardous*

your breathing steadies
as it deepens
and called to being
          under breathing's incantation
delicate scents rise from your body
as you sleep, like little fires

breaking
on a mountainside.
This transmutation manifests
in subtle fragrances, resinous
          or floral—or, tonight: a citrus
softened with aloe, spreads
along your shoulder, down
the shallow canyon
of your spine
down
to where my arm is curved
around your waist
          —very still
very careful
not to wake you
from your alchemy

A story filmed
in California (aliens

devouring New York
again) tours

the straightedge states
and swells the cinemas

in Texas. And for
an hour, Texans

are amused, transported
to that fantastic

Other America—taken in
by images sent back

from that country
where their soybeans

and their methane go.
But often now

for Texans, California
is just a major

motion picture, New York
little different than

Disney World—places
nice to visit, sure,

but a body
could never really live there

I often find I'm looking back
or looking over blinding snow
or looking with a lazy eye

and if I could simply turn around
or fully wake
or open all my other eyes

then I would see with certainty
the world is filled with God
and God with the world,

that God is pregnant with the world.
It ought to be so obvious, if only
I could receive my sight. I wonder

if the End of Time is God
giving birth—as Mary
once gave birth to God?

God, intent and laboring
All His Eyes
unwilling to look away

Hush! What is She murmuring,
the Moon in the milky sky?
She's singing a song she heard from the Sun:

His daylight lullaby

Hush! What are they saying,
the Stars in their shimmering crowds?
They're telling the tales they hear from the Moon

whispered above the clouds

Hush! Where are they going,
the Planets in grand parade?
They carry the wisdom of Stars to the dawn

where night must meet the day

Hush! It's nearly morning.
The Sun will soon appear
shining with stories the Planets composed for Him

Listen, and you'll hear

Out of deference, I lend
a little ear or eye,
but Sight I send

on journeys up or in to find
where center is periphery,
where heart is mind.

Out of courtesy, I make
a little bow, not insincere,
to religion or technology.

          But here
where you might recognize a face
isn't where a Self is anchored.

Even as we speak, I sail
over seas of conversation
to that Great Embrace

It was really the First Supper
so (as with all new things)
there was some confusion
about protocol. A certain amount
of grubbing and reaching. Side

conversations and a looming
tension quite cluttered the mood.
Here was God   God!
offering a strangely simple meal

of earth and sky. Here were day
and night and disciples, all
in a room—an upper room,
which means suspended
which means disbelief

of a sort. Let's say, instead,
varied levels of belief. Judas gawks
greedily at the onions; Thomas
doubts the quality of the wine.

But representing the opposite
extreme: Saint John: who presses
his ear so close   so close!
so he can, without distraction,
hear God's *Let There Be*

gravy and veal and blintzes, because
he knows there are no Seconds
(a Next Supper, feathered and opulent)
until the First has been consumed

When Adam traded
for the apple, God

had angels wrap the world
in a silver tablecloth

and taught Adam manners
in place of mysteries, digestion

instead of indulgence. This fork
and plate are morality and

religion; ruminating keeps you
nourished and disciplined.

Now, said God, you've chosen
a difficult meal. But

when you've finished skin
and pulp and seed, the fructose

with the cyanide, I will make
your bed and pour the wine

of sleep. Tomorrow is time
for better beginnings, so

Adam, when you wake,
remember: eat Life (not less)

and be careful to distinguish Food
from the husk that hides it

Go today to dig your grave.
Choose a lonely place.
Measure first; dig mindfully.

Restrain your thoughts, because your memory must be free
to dig a hollow parallel, to inter a record of soil types, of smells
and of humidity at various depths. Which roots of which trees?
What sizes of stones? What artifacts have been unearthed?

Be gentle with the roots; scatter the stones. Consider: you yourself
are so much earth displaced. Consider the volume of your grave.
Your height and breadth are two of its dimensions. Depth however,
is determined by your endurance, which is the wisdom embedded

in your will. Know that your measurement requires both a symbolic
Unit and a symbolic Number of units. A ration and a ratio. Know
why you make these choices, even if the answer is: I feel, but can't
explain. Because when you finish digging, you'll be looking down

> at the end of explanation
> at the end of excuse
> at the end of blind enjoyment.

Then go back to your life. Go back to home and job and family, to
internet and sex and conversation, to habits and addictions. You'll find
that these things, which once gripped you tightly, have lost their hold.
Now, there are (beneath all busyness, beneath all daily noise) the hollow

in the earth and the hollow in your memory. Confined in burial,
you are free. Let joy be joy and grief be grief: temporary, not to be
embraced or avoided. Your numerology and your symbolic measurement
—a cubit, a fathom, the fraction of a li—is all around you, making

> every door an invitation
> every meal a requiem
> every hope a eulogy

Silver chalice
tarnished, resting
on two stems

bearing two handles &
engraved with symbols

of divinity. Pierced
by seven vents, vapors
of the Elixir of Life

enter freely, so thirst
and satiety might
conjoin. Darkly bright

within & seen
only by the Drinker:

a single ruby,
mounted on posts
of gold

Today the Sun descends
to embrace the Moon.

He abandons all appearances:
His grandeur, His warmth,
His blazing light.

These are His veils
of myth. In their place,
He takes up helplessness. He

takes up nudity. He takes up
wintertime. As water sinks
into thirsty soil, the Moon

receives Him. As fire cleaves
to fuel, so fuel becomes fire:

His infinite suddenness
Her eternal surprise

In holy dark, on shoulder blades, on pottery
and tortoise shells, I grave the attributes of God

and number all His Names. A glowing iron
plied against these fresh inscriptions splits

the glassy surface of the bones
with forks of lightnings and a *crackle* echoes
through the secret room. A net

of paths appears, connecting Names and Symbols
— a design disguised as chance —
to indicate the answer Heaven's will ordains.

By careful art, I read the whole
or broken lines, and in them see the shades
and lights which make the Book

of Changes. Drinking Tao and Te, I prophecy
by gifts of signs and splintered sound

I'm no atheist. God
can tell me secrets
if He wants to. But

I don't easily adjust
to new information. I hope
(mostly for His sake)

He doesn't need me
to respond with happy
surprise. I have my routine.

So God can tell me secrets
if He likes, but I'm crowded
with so much other, prior

faith and obligations,
so full already, that a secret
won't mean much.

I'd rather have
something practical, if God
feels a need to share. Advice.

Or a simple rule.
Rules are helpful.
I'll complain of course — my *God!*

Another *rule*? But, to be honest,
I prefer lists
to intimacies. Besides,

what would I do
with a secret from God?
Some giddy whisper?

Some revelation unbounded?
I'd rather keep a clear,
functional distance.

But it's up to Him.

I'm no atheist

Why aren't they holding hands?
a girl asks her father
squinting curiously up at the ceiling
of the Sistine Chapel. And following
her eyes, I look above the tourists' heads
to where, like film stills cut

from a reel and spread in place
of Heaven: images I've seen
reproduced in kitsch, in textbooks,
in satire. But especially, those
famously sinuous hands (thought
reaching or receding, but in truth

immobile) with a gulf of unpainted plaster
fixed between them. Why aren't they
touching? The girl's question a stimulant
or a solvent. For which unfortunate Age
is this uncompleted reach
a satisfying portrait

of human origins? It's not
the ancient story, the birth from virgin
earth and Spirit, Birth in wonder
out of Wonder. God as Adam's
anchorage; Adam as God's Heart's
concern. Creation is not *other*

than God. It delights Him and it
costs. Adam summoned always
from God's boiling blood; Incarnation
intimate as a spear-thrust; Adam within God,
engraved on every rib. Instead,
the Sistine ceiling shows a novel deity,

muscular and indifferent, the sign
of a culture legislating its release
from the divine entwining. Muscular
and indifferent theologies and sciences
are what it wants. Humanity now self-complete,
its god looks on approvingly

from afar. I confess, I'm shaken. How
did we never see dismemberment in God
taken out of Adam, Adam out of God?
The monstrous gap
between those frescoed fingers is a surgery
cauterizing as it vivisects; it leaves us

numb to the extent of loss. *Adam,*
where are you? Crowds of Adam's children
amble through the Chapel, past the eyes
of languid guards. Does anyone see? A girl
in a blue dress with a red scarf
has broken the illusion

Carmine / Indigo
        blood
departing, returning
urgent errands for the heart

Ruby / Diamond
        lanes
of traffic fly
night's long highways

Olivine / Citrine
        leaves
Autumn shyly
emerges in an Aspen grove

Gold / Lead
        sunrise
facing East
my shadow heavy behind me

Carmine / Indigo
        shifts
of galaxies
as light expands and speaks

Loki came over tonight
to sell me a column of air.
I'm so trusting; I let him in.
I was thinking of you—your
lips, actually—and Loki

is an ancient salesman. He knows
the business. So at that moment
he had your lips. Of course, it was
just an illusion, I know, but it
startled me into a blushing

befuddlement. I said *Oh… sure?*
when he said *Hey there!*
Can I come in, just for a bit?
I blushed because blood
always rushes to my skin

when you're around. (You blush
the color of velvet yarrow. I noticed
but forgot to tell you.) Anyway,
I listened to Loki go on for an hour
about air, and searched his face

for more of yours. I wanted him
to have your hands or your eyes
or to leave. It made me ache
painfully for you. And Loki
used my pain to his advantage

I spend a lot of time
down here on the subway.

To work and back.
To movies and bars.   And I once

ran into God.   This happened
before I really knew my way around.

I had a lot of questions
(obviously) but what I really needed was

        direction.
We discussed possible routes.   And
in the end, He pointed me towards Eden.

He hinted that it wasn't so far, or
(He said) why was there any enjoyment

in life at all?   Microbrews and sex and
thunderstorms—all are drifts of levity

        from Paradise.
Now, the best way for you (He said)

is to marry Eve.   She's My glory
personified, drawn out, made

tactual. How? I asked. He suggested
        we throw a dinner party

and invite all our best friends,
who might also be our children.

You'll continually astound each other.
You won't need television. Everywhere

is the kitchen. Prayer and love (He said)
      aren't separate errands. What if

someday, morning light came in
at once through every window? I still

think about that advice, that direction
God gave me a while ago.

I think about it while the subway
clatters. Lights flutter.
      To work and back

No atmosphere. She had to hold
her breath to keep from laughing.

Only silt and stones. She'd spread
a cloak of dust to dim her music.

Men of earth expect more earth,
She reasoned. What else can they

recognize? The ancients, though!
The ancients needed no machines;

She offered her Elixir freely then.
The childlike still catch Her in a game

of chase. Even at a distance, that
milk-and-ivory smile. Unmistakable.

We need only ask, and the dust is lifted.
Only trust, and the song returns

The ancients needed no machines

Folderol! Shenanigans!
The Devil dances widdershins
and grates against the saint and sage;

the Devil races, retrograde.
            Baselard and Blunderbuss!
The Devil's devils hiss and fuss

and spin ellipses crossed and cursed
while blades are drawn and bullets burst.
            Laudanum and Chloroform!

The Devil chants a tritone chord
to dim the ear and blur the eyes;
the Devil's victims mesmerized.

            Malediction! Pestilence!
The Devil thrives at our expense;
he spreads the cholic and the pox

to celebrate the equinox.
            Toxicant Gastronomy!
on bitter bread and nettle tea

the Devil feeds, and drops the crumbs
to chambermaids and scullions.
            Cinderella! Goldilocks!

The Devil mutters counter-clocks;
he tells the stories end to start
with villains in the hero's part.

            Blasphemy! Cacophony!
The devil weaves his sophistry
in circles with a fire behind

to make the wicked wheel unwind—
   Crinkum-crankum! Caterwaul!
   Shenanigans and Folderol!

and when the wheel is wound again
in eels' coils and serpents' skins
   then *Folderol! Shenanigans!*

the Devil dances widdershins

In the last third of the night
        (so says the hadith)
the Exalted descends to the earthly heaven
        and stands among the stars
                as a gardener stands
among immaculate rows of flowers.
        And the Exalted says:

        Does anyone call me?
                I am here.
        Does anyone have a need?
                I will give.
        Does anyone cry out
                to be forgiven?
                        I am here with nothing
                        but forgiveness.

In the last third of the night
a sleeping soul hears that Voice
in its dream. And perhaps
        into the world of the dream
        a Syllable enters
is taken and remade by the dream
                        into a dream-thing:
        a hallway
        a face
        a child's toy
        or a garden   so full of that Voice

that the sleeping soul longs for Names and Needs
and Sins
enough to wake
an endless   *yes*

Envy will be federally enforced.

Along with taxes, lust will be assessed:
preference(s) and orientation(s)

listed after date of birth. Do you
watch enough pornography?

Toward which celebrities do you direct
your healthy need to obsess? Those

who fail to take their antidepressants
or to frequently update their social media

will be placed on an automated watchlist.
For suspect persons [suspicious activity

may include: infrequent internet use,
infrequent condom purchases, etc.] helpful

hormones will be prescribed and therapy
recommended or required. Activism

will be encouraged toward approved causes.
An unmodern ethic destabilizes the economy.

Education programs are now in place

What is skin? We can't decide. A boundary or
a wedding dress? Yours has remarkable coherence:

the skin of your hands and the skin beneath your breasts:
hickory. Maplewood? Himalayan salt. I think about melanin

and the subterranean shade of roaming blood that makes skin
so bewildering. I reach for your hand. I reach for words, but

language was invented by men—men in long robes
and sandaled feet, with eager bodies and wiry beards (men

on whom the statues of Sumerians and Phoenicians
were modeled). So language is *clothed*, and not a little

blind. It has no exposure. Contentment? Exultation.
Only metaphors and referents. I could watch television.

I could stream pornography. But this would just be
nouns and verbs. Motion pictures. Only screens,

not skin. Not practical. Glorified? Unspeakable.
Always a caress or a death away from definition

In the beginning was the Tao
And the Tao knew the Tao
And the Tao breathed the Tao

    And the Tao said, We
    will make an infinity
    between Tao and Tao

    We will reach across
    from Tao to Tao. We
    will draw Tao into Tao

    And the Tao made Yang
    and the Tao made Yin
    to enjoy the Union of Tao

the Ten Thousand Things
originate in Yang,
find perfection in Yin
and return to Yang

    And the Tao left the Tao
    without leaving. Opened
    to receive Yang and Yin

    without opening. And
    the Tao said, Now I am
    the Yang and the Yin:

    Non-made Creature,
    Non-creating Maker,
    the chasm and the bridge

And the Tao breathed all things
And the Tao knew all things.
In the ending was the Tao

almost never almost never
yellow birds in nests of heather
yellowed books
        in gilded leather

faintly shining faintly shining
sky's a silver necklace winding
with its pearls
        of stars aligning

ever secret ever secret
warm and dark the deserts keep it
all the wealth
        of ancient Egypt

very seldom very seldom
sycamores with vines to belt them
in their shade
        a rose is sheltered

        so it seems love so it seems
        never sounds like what it means
        this is how they rhyme in dreams

only rarely only rarely
heart's a heavy weight to carry
with her griefs
        that wake so early

Because there isn't any history
I've made plans to sail
to enter stealthily those undying lands
where Boadicea and Cleopatra
meet for tea. They rise
to greet the entrance of Diaochan
the dancing girl, heroine
of Three Kingdoms
and Parvati, who won her god
by raw austerities.

I've made plans to sail, because
I want to know the Secret
such sublime women gather
to discuss. Or if
since there isn't any history
must their meeting always and forever
have no agenda, no men, no need
for secrets

Let's begin with the Sun
and follow on from Him
to other religious ideas.

The Sun is a door, oculus
and aperture of Release.
Climbing the ladder of light,

we pass though, unbound.
The Sun is differently
composed than has been

reported lately: smaller
than the palm of a hand
(hold up your hand

to compare). And the Sun
isn't yellow. Look quick:
He flashes: blue-red-black.

And not a globe, He's
the glint at one point
of a hollow sphere,

a heaven, within which
we are wandering now.
The Sun indicates

the boundary (perhaps
otherwise invisible)
of this sphere, the limit

of one mode of life. He
defines *time*; He defines
death; He defines *exit*.

To accept is to ascend is
to expand. When you find
your Way within this series

of inversions, your departure
through the Sun Door
sets this heaven inside you

Between the mountains Not-yet-
knowing-need & Wanting-what-

you-have-and-are is this Valley
of Compulsive Envy. I simply

call it Hell. But I'm no longer
desperate to escape. You see,

I've lived here for many years
& I can't be fooled. I know

the secret. I know desperation
is just another of its tortures

A narrow, curving path
lightly veiled under willow leaves
leads from an unpaved road
to the side of Saint Michael's Spring.

The old wooden gate left open
and a sandstone boulder are your signs.
From early Spring to middle Autumn,
wild hops and lacevine follow you

down to where the water swells
at the feet of sleepy Cottonwoods.
You hear them lean together, giants
whispering about the rain

above the shady clearing. There,
circled with stones to embellish
her small simplicity, a cast and painted
Virgen de Guadalupe

greets Saint Michael's thirsty guests.
The cinnamon-hue of her skin
and turquoise of her faded robes
are spread with stars—each star

the pale concrete shimmering
where a fleck of paint was chipped away
by frost or wind. You arrive
from the long afternoon, thirsty

with an unspoken hope.
You know the place by its wooden gate,
by Nuestra Señora's open hands and
by an amber silence, which playfully
         at intervals
the music of the water breaks

In the Age to Come
or in a Buddha Field or in
the Higher Paradise,

when dead are vested
in clothes re-woven from the
primal Light, how

will the former, mortal
life appear to us in retrospect?
I see it something like

a tiny figure sculpted
in the soul: a Kachina Doll, a
holy toy to teach

and to remind us:
once, we sojourned briefly
through the wilds

at the edge of God.
Once we were divided, far
from Self. Yet

even then, fallen
and fragile, it was a world
of limitless grace

once, we sojourned
briefly through the wilds
at the edge of God

Dramatis Personæ (in order of appearance):
Carl Jung
Housekeeper
Mircea Eliade

Scene: *Carl Jung's garden in late Spring. Clothing and furniture appropriate to the German intellectual/leisure class, circa 1956. Above, creating a canopy for the action of the play, a spacious apple tree, buoyant with rose-pink blooms, spreads over the stage. Below, various flowers (some referenced in the dialogue) adorn the stage floor. A holly hedge forms the rear and stage-left boundaries of the garden. To stage-right is the back door of the Jung house.*

Furnishings: *two cedar-plank garden chairs. Perhaps a small table between. Carl Jung employs a blackthorn walking cane.*

Tone of the dialogue: *serious, yet light-hearted as befits old friends who respect each other while disagreeing at many points; academic, but not confined to academia. In the privacy and trust of friendship, the characters are somewhat vulnerable and playfully combative.*

[*Lights rise to reveal* **Carl Jung** *reading a newspaper in the stage left garden chair silently, a cane propped up beside him. The* **Housekeeper** *enters from stage right and crosses to Jung, pointing back toward the house. Carl nods, and stands expectantly, leaning on his cane as the Housekeeper departs. A moment later, the Housekeeper returns, leading* **Mircea Eliade***, and gestures toward Carl Jung. Eliade and the housekeeper bow. The Housekeeper exits.*]

Carl Jung: My friend! You haven't changed; you look as if the years have hardly disturbed you. Perhaps your hair is whiter? White as the Moon in Dostoevsky's dream. How long has it been?

[*Carl indicates the otherchair, nearest the house. Mircea sits, slightly facing stage left. Carl remains standing or walking, gesturing throughout the discussion.*]

Mircea Eliade: Since before the War. Though many wars have come and gone in our days. And many more will come, I suppose.

Jung: Yes, the War. This garden was once a battlefield, you know. I sometimes think of all the wars—the Norse and Germanic, and the Modern, pushing territory boundaries back and forth over what are now my cucumber beds.

Eliade: Like human tides among the hills and fields. I wonder what secrets your garden hides beneath these lovely flowers?

Jung: Bones and armor tangled in the roots of hyacinths.

Eliade: Bullets just below the clover and the chicory.

Jung: Arrowheads beside lost wedding rings? But tell me, what brings you to the battlefield in this moment free from war—when we have a little space and a little time to watch the birds and think the best of our humanity?

Eliade: A lecture tour, and a chance to see old friends. But particularly, I am intrigued about your current project. In our correspondence, you spoke of a preface or introduction you were adding to the translation of a Chinese text? You must tell me more! You said, enigmatically, 'it's important to remember we can never find a satisfying home on Earth.' Please do continue.

Jung: Ah, yes. With all its beauty, we can never sleep here peacefully: Earth is a merciless bed. A mother who threatens—even eats—her children. She gives a life its day and then, as if dissatisfied, aborts what she's produced and sketches out the forms again and again.

Eliade: Variations on the sparrow?

Jung: Adaptations of the cottonwood.

Eliade: Reinventions of the lands and seas.

Jung: So why do we, here in the West of the world, study these ephemeral, fragile things? We paint a still-life. We look for 'force' in physics. We examine single *frames* of the film reel. But it's *change* —

the rapid change from frame to frame—that gives the pictures life-like motion! The Western mind considers objects, ideas in isolation. The East, in contrast, ponders moments of transition, moments we might call Archetypes of Instability. Our ancient inspirations gave us very different courses: the Orient examines kinds of Change; the Occident attempts to map the Forms.

Eliade: Where did these ancient inspirations come from?

Jung: Or our own, our current inspirations? I myself have wasted so much youth in chasing what I thought were fixed ideas, I fear I spoiled the fruit by tasting it too soon.

Eliade: Yes, inspiration comes less quickly now, but when it comes, it comes with quiet power. No longer does it bear the stamp of fantasy, but—and here I disagree with you—inspiration seems to rise now out of Earth Herself. Not the cannibal which you describe: an older Earth, accustomed to converse with Heaven.

[*The Sun, unveiled for a moment, shines on the apple tree. A warm light increases slightly over the stage.*]

Jung: How unexpected, but most welcome! Our alpine Spring has few moments of sunshine. Look how the light shimmers on the apple leaves and on the flowers.

Elaide: As if answering the stars.

[*A gentle wind disturbs the branches of the garden trees. Apple petals fall.*]

Jung: [*Brushing petals from his hair, laughing*] The Sun seems every year to retire into a state of contemplation. We call it Winter. He retires from His work of warming us so we will be reminded of our dependence on Him and, I think, so He will be reminded of his dependence on the very nature of Being.

Eliade: And maybe He regains His strength through contemplation? With Spring as his enlightenment?

Jung: Very silly, of course, and not compatible with science. Yet there's something in it.

Eliade: Yes. The apocalyptic nature of appearances. We might say it's the *appearance* of the body, not anatomy, which confirms the body bears a soul. How the body 'works' is, of course, important. But the surface symmetry of the human face is the deeper revelation.

Jung: We still say 'sunset' though we claim to believe the Earth goes around the Sun.

[*The men are silent for a moment, pondering the disconnect between belief and sense and fact.*]

Eliade: Thinking of the ancient model of the universe against the modern reminds me of our old disagreement.

Jung: Regarding at what level our souls connect with what is greater than ourselves?

Eliade: Yes. You've written of a Collective Unconscious, a murky aquifer from which we all can draw, from which creativity emerges. I sense—I see—instead, a Great Return. A share in a reality far wider than ourselves but from which we are inseparable.

Jung: A murky aquifer? I would say, rather, we are digging in ourselves for fossils buried there since the dawn of human self-awareness.

Eliade: My experience suggests it is we who are fossils. Or rather, the gemstones. Precious stones in a cosmic mine, raw and buried, capable of bearing light; but cold and dark until we're found and claimed and cut and fixed in golden settings—fit adornments for the gods. Why should we dig, when we are dug for? Search blindly when we are sought?

Jung: Searched for by the gods? An inverted prayer?

Eliade: Prayer, intuition, is not a child's puzzle. Prayer is courage to leap or to be thrown into the fire and forged anew. Prayer is reconnection with the permanent, the Origin.

Jung: My dear Mircea! I cannot quite agree with you. The world is spread before me. Nothing is forbidden, nothing wasted. My inner life suggests I should leap out–not into the hands of Myth, however true, but into the unformed void. My reason and my memory and my imagination all in concert say, Partake! Consume! Participate! The world is formless until we give it form. Except when conscience checks, I plan to take and taste and learn. Are religion and philosophy just the closing up of life in morals? Or do they set free the soul for greatness it otherwise could not know?

Eliade: I understand the lure, the love for new experience and as-yet-unknown pleasures of the mind. But the world is *written*. It has a grammar. You cannot simply overwrite; you must listen first, and then become a poet. The prophets and the sages never spoke of what they imagined, but of what they *saw*. Ezekiel's wheels-within-cosmic-wheels; Elijah's fiery chariot flying. Heraclitus and Laotzu planned their lasting city modelled on the Logos and the Tao.

Jung: But you would accuse me of knowing only Cain in exile? Only Jeremiah's Heaven-rending lamentations? Only "Why have you forsaken me?" never "I commit my Spirit to Your care?"

Eliade: Of course, it's not so simple. There are no dichotomies except in politics! How can I tell you what I see? Perhaps each soul chooses different instruments for its research. You have an hourglass. And gazing though it back to ancient times you see yourself usefully distorted by its narrow oculus and curving bulb. I am lifting up a sextant. I hold it to the sky and measure Earth against the Stars. [*they pause to consider this image.*] A Hindu myth explains this more clearly than I could. Do you know the Story of the Birds from the Upanishad?

Jung: Please remind me.

Eliade: Your 'Unconscious' and my 'Return' are not compatible, yet they're inseparable. A tension stands between them, joining them. One is Hermes, one is Aphrodite. Who can say? Yet we have a simple tale, very old, painted by the manuscript illuminators, woven into tapestries, carved in light relief on wood and stone: Twin Birds in the branches of a spacious Tree. The year is late, the Tree is filled with fruit. One Bird flits from branch to branch, testing, tearing, intent at every taste. The other simply waits, observes. "Here are limbs and leaves and light," he says, "and Self." This second Bird does not eat, he looks. He looks deeply. And his contemplation leads him beyond the Tree, upward, to the life-creating Sun.

Jung: To a kind of stillness beyond all movement?

Eliade: Ah! That's very interesting. Could it be that it is not in motion or in static things—but in 'a stillness beyond all movement' that we find the key to other Ages, other ways of Being?

Jung: This would bring together what—[*the sound of voices echoes suddenly from the direction of the house. The Housekeeper appears, approaches Carl Jung, speaks silently to him. Jung answers Eliade's unspoken question:*]—Journalists! I forgot I told them they could come today for an interview. We must pause our conversation for the moment. All things end, I do suppose. Even the best of things.

Eliade: Atlantis was subsumed by rising seas.

Jung: The Chinese sages flourished while their nation fractured into Warring States.

Eliade: The Golden Age of Athens lasted less than fifty years!

Jung: This won't take long. Then we can resume our conversation, perhaps with a meal? I'll step inside to give you some quiet. Such is the price of publication, these interruptions. Please enjoy the garden, and I'll have tea brought out in a moment. There's a lovely road just beyond the gate if you'd care to take a walk.

Eliade: Just beyond the gate! Ah, what then?

Jung: Patience and courage are required. We can't alleviate, but we can staunch and medicate and carry on.

Eliade: The pain remains; the wound will always weep.

Jung: Always. With longing, perhaps.

[*Carl departs. Mircea sits quietly for several moments, eyes closed. Wind again stirs the garden as two holly trees part slightly to reveal a wooden gate, stage left, previously hidden. Mircea looks up. He sees the gate. He stands, slowly and rather stiffly. Apple blossoms fall from his lap.*]

Eliade: Dostoevsky dreamt about the Moon breaking. Winter lingers overlong. The drought seems interminable. And the heart mourns until she finds the hidden gate, and reaches for the rusted hinge, the heavy latch. Yes, what then...? [*He walks toward the gate, opposite the direction of the house. He reaches for the handle.*] Is this the mystery...? [*Mircea turns the handle with a quiet click and a pleasant creaking of hinges. He is surprised for a moment how easily it opens.*] One simply opens a door, and passes to the other side.

[*He departs. Wind again. Light brightens for a moment as before, then dims slowly to dark.*]

Fin.

Since the drought, the sound of rain

is like a guest arriving late
who brings a rare liqueur to share,
pouring everyone a generous cup

Since the drought, the sound of rain

is like the heavy cold
of that trophy we trained for, showered
with cheers from a delighted crowd

Since the drought, the sound of rain

is like the incense breathed back
from church walls on a warm afternoon
when I'm alone and listening

Since the drought, the sound of rain

is like the face of my friend
who died five years ago, her smile returning
a pledge of resurrection

Since the drought, the sound of rain
is, most of all, my son

who woke like thunder from a fevered sleep
and in a joyful torrent, tried
to tell me all his dreams at once

For Glasir the Golden Tree; for Avalon,
the Isle of Apple Flowers; for   Elysium of Artemis,
and Aaru,   Egyptian paradise of wild game

For Agartha underground, for Jannah
of the Sufis;   Krishnaloka,   gods' abode of love;
for El Dorado and Atlantis. For those yet-living

stones of Lalibela;   yes,   for even Numinor and
the Silver Sea of liquid light,   and for that
childhood forest   where I found a hidden cave

but was afraid   to go inside.   For cities which
are   gardens, too, in union.   Dripping myrrh,
   streets of glass,   mountains of spices. For

   silence so profound, it sings. Whether these
are dreams or myths, I can't discern.   Dare I hope
they might be   *memories?*   For each, and

for them all at once, I find
                                   no relief from longing

They might be memories?

Take up again your sitting. Dōgen
suggests the early light, and writes
you won't wait long

before the Jackals begin spying
from the forest shadows
of your stomach, from the rumbling

traffic of unfinished chores. Jackals
surround you to devour you
with distraction. Dōgen suggests

do nothing. Though your brain
explodes with imagery. Has a bed
been left for you in place

of the ancient altar? Which
is the real midnight? Whose are
these tentacled mangroves? Yalps

and yells of the Jackals. Dōgen
already warned you how the many
converge into the Great Jackal,

described how you slide
along the cloud-like lines
of its iris, into the pit

of your own imagination.
Do nothing. An incessant melody.
A technicolor memory. A solution for

that nagging dilemma. Do nothing.
Patient unconcern is your posture.
Dōgen says don't be fooled:

all your thought is Jackal, just
as all you see in sleep is dream.
For the sitting hour,

you sit. Sitting is its own
enlightenment. In fear of flames
that guard the gates of Paradise,

the Jackals wish to lead you
far from your heart. But you
defy them, daring to be burned

I was betrothed to Beauty
and married young, with years
of youth ahead. But I began
to age, while Beauty kept

her agile grace. I could have
asked for her secret. Instead,
I wanted to exhaust her
with my apologies and my

pains, refusing the invitations
she never ceased to extend.
She loved the out-of-doors,
but I wanted her to fade

proudly with me in front
of the television, never far
from the thermostat. She
refused. In Winter, she is

ever delighted by the snow,
and in Summer still flies
around our garden, scolding
the bluejays and brushing

her lips against that stubborn
jimsonweed—the one I hate
and tried to poison, the one
coming back year after year

in the poor soil under our
bedroom window. Year after year
more lush, as if to mock me
with its endurance. It spends

its albedo carelessly, pouring out
its ethereal libations
in an effusion of waste
like an ignorant child

Within its morning wash
the Universe is satisfied. Our bedroom
          is a basket of clothes
of chairs and books. The nearest

is the book I read to you last night
          —about the temple builders
who enshrine their gods
in alabaster. It turned your dream

          into the story of a cavern
where laundry is sorted. You
are the Sibyl who separates
by color and by type of cloth,

who chooses sacred stones
to pound the laundry clean.
You laugh aloud, alone, because
          this stone: *did it imagine*

in all its subterranean years
that such things as fabrics and dyes exist?
Such things as the ritual of washing?
Or that it would itself be smoothed

and polished by something
          soft as laundry?
And you wake up laughing, to tell me
the Universe is satisfied, because

its dreams are mended—some
the scattered, some the sorted, some
          the neatly folded dreams.
          These last: the dreams
which you and I will wear today

It isn't that I don't believe. It's just
there's too much to believe. I take my meds.
I try to limit fats and screen-time. If it isn't
raining, I take walks. For exercise. Not far,
but always on a way I like to go.

I think about God sometimes while I walk,
and church. There's a church along my road.
They used to have a little garden and beautiful
stained glass windows before they renovated.
They used to have a Cross out front, but they

replaced it with a notice board. There's a cat
who comes over from my neighbor's apartment.
She's very friendly; I save milk and table scraps
to give her. She seems happy, so content.
Sometimes I watch her sleep. Sometimes I look

for signs of God, for proofs in small things.
In cats' faces. In flowers. At that church,
I hear drums and laughter when I walk by
on Sunday mornings. I think: on Sundays
maybe God is closer then. I listen sometimes

to the wind or to the traffic. Listening, I guess,
for a sound that only God could make. Or
a beautiful coincidence. Or something old
that's still around, forgotten—like something
that might have once belonged to God

Call me home by miracles
I must be lonely to receive.

Call me in the quiet dark
of grief, and in the tension

of my lust. And long before
my list of chores can cause

my pride to swell. Call me when
I see the Moon against blue skies;

call me on the greyest days (in
February often, please). Call me

by the gentle wind that follows
on a hurricane. And on the

anniversaries of losses. Call me
with caresses. Call me home

with beer and conversation.
Call me up with angels'

trumpets; all the sooner, if I fall
to sleeping (in that driest, coldest

sleeping) call me home by miracles
shining in that isolated hour

Sunlight is a child sleeping
just inside my window
on the floor beneath the table
where I keep my cup and book.

Sunlight like a child throws
his body whole-self into sleep
as if into another game. What is joy
but self-forgetfulness fulfilled in

a contented rest? And who could rest
more joyfully than light? Silent,
sleeping light, you've flown so far!
Eight light-minutes from the Sun!

So I will not disturb your well-earned
sleep. I have no worries that would
wake you, no concerns today, no tasks
except my quiet book. Its turning

pages sound like oak leaves pattering
along the sidewalk, whispering
a Winter incantation. The easing
of its spine is branches sighing

in a Summer wind. I know it's just
an idle book. But its rhymes are full
of pictures, and its rhythms imitate
the breath of sleeping light

I imagined us
at the Shoe Tree in Nevada
or at Stauf's, Grandview, behind
my childhood home on the Bank Block
          tangling our shoes
          sampling local pastry

I imagined we're wandering
the Missouri River Breaks
in rented canoes, or drinking
the absolute silence
of that historic library
          you spot an eagle
          I find the right book

And I imagined, without intending to,
you waking me
with a furtive hand at 3 am
and I am willing, because
          this is knowledge
          we only have tonight

But since I know
we never have what we imagine,
I don't speak. I say nothing.
So that you,
          without suspecting,
leave behind all this imagination.
          a world discarded
          a wreckage
          an abandoned life

On the vertical: *Reason & Mystery.*
On the horizontal: *What you can't know*
& What you can't help
knowing. This diagram has space

for what you see yet don't understand and
what you understand but can't explain,
nearer one or another pole, toward or away
from the Center.

But the Center is not merely a point
among potentials. The Center may be
a glass of salted orange juice — which
you won't appreciate until you're lost

in Bangkok on a muggy afternoon.
The Center is where obscure, unplottable
events and questions arise, the questions
rarely asked, such as: what to do when life

takes away your lemons? Such as: is it ok
to count your chickens before they hatch
if all your eggs are in one basket? Rarely
do two wrongs make a right. But frequently

three rights make a left
when driving San Francisco's labyrinth
of one-ways. Such as: why is grapefruit
contraindicated by your father's

heart medication? With each question
you come closer to that placeless
Center. Out of *Reason* and out
of *Knowing,* both. Out in

Kansas City, which used to seem
so unfamiliar. Until one Summer
charged it all with such exquisite
nostalgia.   When you find

your moment on the Diagram, you find
a third axis (yours, uniquely) on which
there's no room, no *where,* for confusion
or anxiety: such as: at the grocery store

that time you were fifteen
and mortified, because you had to ask
the attractive clerk, *Excuse me.*
But do you have any kumquats?

When I asked why, my father said
The world is flat
compared with your capacity to receive it.

When I asked how so, he said
Remember the old story. Everything
is supported on the back

of a very careful elephant
who stands with stupendous balance
on the scaly shell

of a very patient tortoise.
Then he laughed, and explained
For the symbolists

and the myth-minders among us
the meaning of the image is clear.
He spread his wide arms

and raised his voice
All things huge and loudly *manifest*
and whispering, continued

Rely upon the strong and *secret.*
When I seemed confused, he added
The ponderous heft of animal physics

—quanta and eros and effort—stands
with stupendous balance
on the subtle web of something *other,*

something much more Real.
Then almost to himself he said
It's good to remember, as the elephant does,

beneath the flapping ears and pounding legs
of trumpet-blaring Everyday, another Life
is hiding. Another *kind* of life,

you understand? A life
that, in comparison, makes this one seem
preliminary. Thin, and papery. In music,

in morning light, in grieving, too,
this other Life is sometimes glimpsed
and can be grasped. But

you must be prepared for it. Then
he sighed (as if remembering)
From time to time, the tortoise

emerges from its shell
to find out what you're ready to receive.
And as it slips away again inside itself,

invites you, winking (or was
my father winking?), you can leave
the paper world. Don't dismiss

the Myths, my father used to say.
Science and Poetry are lovers,
only lately estranged

I am not a cat
person. I am
simply a cat.

I strategize, or
I nap. I ignore,
or I know

with uncanny
clarity. Perhaps
I will break

this cup. Then
disappear into
my secrets. I

quietly watch
the birds, or
eat one. I am

a cat. You
may offer me
your predictions

I ignore
or
I know

I told myself   the story I am.
How once upon a time, I, the Yin Point,

left the Yang Field   of the Taijitu to see
the Ten Thousand Things, and so became

the pupil of a girl's eye.   And in seeing, fell
upon the mark below a handsome mouth. And

being caught   by beauty, was
the end of an exclamation; in hoping, was

the full stop of   an unasked question.
And knowing loss, was the drain of a clawfoot

bathtub in an   abandoned house.
In loneliness, a petrosphere buried on

a Scottish hill;   in bearing history,
Servilia's infamous pearl; in suffering oblivion,

the vacant center   of a chariot wheel.
And knowing anger, was a cannonball exploding

through the timber   of a warship,
breaking eight men's bones. And reddened

with blood,   left wandering, was ten
thousand Apache Tears on a mesa in New Mexico;

emptied by loss,   the lens above
a crowded cinema, projecting motion pictures. Then

tiring of images, became   the halo of darkness
which reveals a star. And for joy, I widened into Night

Herself: all of sky   but only half
of time: archetype of the Yin Field. And looking back

through Yang   to myself in my appointed place, I
recognize the Moon. And I say without speaking, how

am I   the Moon?
I will tell myself the story

Bless the water
Bless the leaves
Bless the empty cup

each gift
its appointed place

Bless the heat
invisible, pulsing
from the heart

each thought
its resolution

Food for the day
A view of the sky
A name for God

in the silence
of imageless prayer

Yi Jing or *The Book of Changes*, a Chinese philosophy outlining universal kinds or contexts of change, has directly influenced the course of events in the Far East for millenia, and has intrigued or baffled generations of European thinkers since its introduction to the West in the early eighteenth century. To oversimplify, *Yi Jing* considers the many confluences of Yang and Yin and represents them in 64 hexagrammic notations of solid (Yang) and dashed (Yin) lines. These 64 direction-possibilites are then described in very earthy language, using images from the natural world, Chinese history, household items and domestic and political relationships.

I first encountered the text during my graduate studies in Far Eastern literature, and since such simple images are also frequently the focus of my own writing, a spontaneous conversation blossomed which became the foundation of this book. Astronomy, religion, light, and the beauty of landscapes are immense subjects to tackle; dialogue with *Yi Jing* furnished both inspiration and limitation. Some of the poems (9, for example) reflect on humorous aspects of the Changes. Some poems are structured according to the numerical value of their hexagrams (11), and some resemble their shape (62). Many have imagery from the *Yi Jing* incorporated into them, and one (32) describes the origin of the hexagrams' symbolic language.

Finally, as the collection came together, I began to consider the contemporary art of filmmaking as a kind of proof or demonstration of change—as the cause or midwife of movement. Before the advent of digital recording, the illusion of motion was achieved by the rapid change from one physical, static image to another—hence the title and the idea of space-time as a cosmic motion picture. My many references to the Moon prompted use of the science fiction classic *Frau Im Mond* (*The Woman in the Moon*) for cover art, and my publisher collected stills to intersperse with the poems in the manner of old "photoplay editions" which were published to promote silent film releases.

Most readers will approach the poems in the usual way, cover-to-cover. This makes the book almost a kind of film. The more adventurous, however, following the custom of *Yi Jing* consultation, might try tossing coins or gathering yarrow stalks and reading the poems in the order thus revealed.

Joshua Alan Sturgill
Feast of Saint Dimitrios, 2022

With deep appreciation

the author acknowledges the following
for previous publication of poems included in this collection:
The Cresset of Valparaiso University;
Forma, the journal of the CIRCE Institute;
Synaxis & **New Moot** of the Eighth Day Institute;
& the online forum of **Darkly Bright Press**

Special thanks are due

to **Marci Rae Johnson** (marciraejohnson@journoportfolio.com)
for inspiration & wise suggestions,
to **Joshua Avni** (jtavni@gmail.com) for his friendship & editorial eye,
to **Tawny Vaughn** (design.tawny@gmail.com)
for this elegant yet dramatic cover, & of course
to my wife, **Rebekah**,
who laughs if the poems are humorous,
nods sagely when they're sobering
& rolls her eyes when I take them too seriously

Interior images from the 1929 film
Frau im Mond

ende

$15.00
ISBN 979-8-9863904-2-0
51500>

www.ingramcontent.com/pod-product-compliance
Lightning Source LLC
Chambersburg PA
CBHW051635120626
46551CB00014B/2085